YOUR KNOWLEDGE HAS VALUE

- We will publish your bachelor's and master's thesis, essays and papers

- Your own eBook and book - sold worldwide in all relevant shops

- Earn money with each sale

Upload your text at www.GRIN.com
and publish for free

Bibliographic information published by the German National Library:

The German National Library lists this publication in the National Bibliography; detailed bibliographic data are available on the Internet at http://dnb.dnb.de .

This book is copyright material and must not be copied, reproduced, transferred, distributed, leased, licensed or publicly performed or used in any way except as specifically permitted in writing by the publishers, as allowed under the terms and conditions under which it was purchased or as strictly permitted by applicable copyright law. Any unauthorized distribution or use of this text may be a direct infringement of the author s and publisher s rights and those responsible may be liable in law accordingly.

Imprint:

Copyright © 2017 GRIN Verlag, Open Publishing GmbH
Print and binding: Books on Demand GmbH, Norderstedt Germany
ISBN: 9783668622890

This book at GRIN:

https://www.grin.com/document/388338

Alaric Naudé

The Naudé Hypothesis. A tool for Semantic Listening

GRIN Publishing

GRIN - Your knowledge has value

Since its foundation in 1998, GRIN has specialized in publishing academic texts by students, college teachers and other academics as e-book and printed book. The website www.grin.com is an ideal platform for presenting term papers, final papers, scientific essays, dissertations and specialist books.

Visit us on the internet:

http://www.grin.com/

http://www.facebook.com/grincom

http://www.twitter.com/grin_com

Title: *The Naudé Hypothesis: A tool for Semantic Listening*
Dr. Alaric Naudé
Professor of Linguistics, Department of Nursing
Suwon Science College, University of Suwon

Abstract: *Newton's Third Law was written as a foundation for much of the understanding of physics. However, the underlying principal of oppositional forces is applicable to various fields of understanding, including the sociolinguistic understanding of semantics. Ethnic groups, governmental forces, institutions of learning and religion all interact to change language and be changed by language itself. While this is a known fact, documenting or understanding the exact interchange and opposition or interaction between two forces has not been sufficiently explored. To facilitate this exploration, the Naudé Hypothesis provides a simplified basis for the theoretical framework and a linguistic model from which to analyse patterns that result from the oppositional forces of two interacting entities in an attempt to understand the meaning behind meanings- semantics.*

Newton's Third law is summarised in the following statement by Newton himself; *Actioni contrariam semper et æqualem esse reactionem: sive corporum duorum actiones in se mutuo semper esse æquales et in partes contrarias dirigi*. Which is to say ; To every action there is always opposed an equal reaction: or the mutual actions of two bodies upon each other are always equal, and directed to contrary parts.

The theory is defined by $F_A = -F_B$ namely that every action has an equal and opposite reaction.

The $F_A = -F_B$ formula will be applied in then be applied to the relation of society to language.

Newton's Third Law has never been invoked in a Linguistic setting. The author however feels that while intended for the field of physics, the structure of the Third Law provides a theoretical basis for Socio-linguistic interactions.

Society influences language and language is in turn an influence on society and this can be measured,

However, this definition albeit pertinent can be problematic when used in a wider sense in that is equates for only two reactionary bodies. In a humanistic sense there are likely to be both supporting and resisting factions or ideals. (Ricento)

In a linguistic sense then actions or even perceived actions can have both a positive or negative influence thereby creating both positive and negative reactions simultaneously. (Wodak)

A different formula based on the Third Law is then proposed in cases that involve situations of comparative support or opposition.

The correct formula in a linguistic sense would then be $F_A = (+F_B) + (--F_B)$.

The first action or series of actions symbolized by F_A will produce complementary actions of similar intensity $(+F_B)$ it will concurrently produce a resisting action ($--F_B$). This formula is purely experimental and needs to be tested.

To illustrate, in a hypothetical situation an institution may choose to change wording within their school motto in order to "modernize" it, this idea may have support due to the progressive nature of individuals and their concepts, yet there may be a resistant force in a more conservative group who object to the change in language for a variety of reasons based on preformed values. In such cases the success of the action is not necessarily bound to a purely democratic process but may be heavily directed by individuals, culture, institutional policies and numerous other factors. The relative outcome be it predominantly $(+F_B)$ or ($--F_B$)will then be based on the combination of various factors not any singular factor.

The dominating set of factors be they $(+F_B)$ or ($-F_B$) will then set the direction for that society on a various linguistic and social issues.

The hypothetical formula will then follow a set of perceivable course.

If $FA =- FB$ then by implication $FA = (+F_B) + (--F_B)$. Further if one side becomes dominant whether $(+F_B)$ or $(--F_B)$, the dominant side becomes an influencing factor on the original FA

In a cycle the F_A will either Galvanise or Undermine the dominant form or group.

To clarify in the form of formula, if $F_A = -F_B$ then in like manner, $F_A =(+F_B) + (--F_B)$. The dominant section will then change the path of the formula. If $FA = (+FB)$ becomes dominant then $F_A = (+F_B)$ in like manner will be $(+F_B) = F_A$.
If $F_A = (-F_B)$then in like manner equates to $(-F_B) = F_A$.

This hypothetical formula will be used to test the relationship between catalyst and language, language and catalyst. It will also be used to compare and collate collected data.

If society influences language, then language in turn influences society.

If a policy is implemented toward language it will be both supported and opposed with the stronger area gaining dominance. Support or Opposition will then will be an influencing factor on language policies either to uphold or degrade the systems under which they hold sway.

In a linguistic sense these "diagnostic artifacts" are references to, and/or literature that displays examples of linguistic shifts, not only in grammar forms used but also in the nature and tone of rhetoric during reforms or social changes or even preceding these so as to gauge the social, political, religious and educational spheres that gave rise to the current system. (Shohamy)

These "diagnostic artifacts" will be analyzed using a comparative framework in which their correlation or lack thereof will the ascertained through the contrast with relative modern or current patterns or linguistic forms.

Examples of this may include the following (this list is by no means exhaustive);

- Frequency of words or idioms

- Deliberate changes to previous forms of wording

- Prohibitions on certain words, expressions or language forms.

- The institution of a "singular" or "authorized" ideas or concepts

which are de rigueur and impose conformity.

- Ways in which the superiority of the current idea system is expounded.

- The degree or force with which language forms are imposed (i.e. the censorship of free speech, prohibition of women to use certain linguistic forms, prohibition of certain groups to point out inconsistencies etc...)

The second area is that of data collection in connection with native speakers and/or experts in the field.

The feelings of native speakers in relation to the "opposing" form of their language can give grounds as to what the proliferated views or institutionalized propaganda that affect the way a particular group or language is perceived really are.

To illustrate, an Institute may say "We have no aversion to dialect B, all dialects are equally acceptable." However, are the views of the members of the given institute in harmony with this principle? Do students through the collected responses show an unbalanced lean toward not using dialect B due to social stigma or the possibility that teachers show favoritism to users of dialect A? Surveyed responses will then give insight not only into "official stances" of institutes or educational systems but rather to the actual situation. This survey will use neutral language to avoid leading to a certain response, it will further choose wording that is culturally sensitive so as to ensure accuracy. Clear identification of any trend or movement toward linguistic discrimination must treated seriously during the stage of data analysis and where this trend originates from, this is because linguistic discrimination is an abuse of human rights. (Rannut)

Data will be interpreted using the traditional forms of data visualization such as graphs depicting the frequencies of results and their interrelated trends. These results will be further used to hypothesize future leaning or directions of societies based on their current linguistic product.

The validity of $F_A = (+F_B) + (-F_B)$ which will henceforth be referred to for the ease of reading and writing as the Naudé Hypothesis.

The test for the Naudé Hypothesis will include the evaluation of the hypothesis through the stability of the results which it produces, or whether the hypothesis produces results that can be measured in any consistent way.

In its construct the hypothesis will seek to identify and categorize the mutational catalysts responsible for the diversity in dialects and for the partiality given to certain dialects within a society.

The danger in this form of hypothetical testing is that of the caveman effect, which leads to an unsatisfactory and inaccurate interpretation of the data in question. (Berk)

Further , due to the complex nature of linguistic influences this formula best serves to explore the relation between two social factors at a time. The formula may be altered to include more fields based on the manner in which the given data is analysed.

Hence, $F_A = (+F_B) + (--F_B)$.

If $\therefore F_A = +F_B$

then it is logical that

$\therefore F_A \neq --F_B$

$+F_B$ and $--F_B$ receive a respective numerical value based on the degree of social dominance they display within the society under observation with a root metric factor of ten being the unit of measurement. The value itself may include decimals although the total value of +10 to -10 may not be exceeded. Exceeding the unitary value of +10 to -10 will indicate an error in the equation sequence.

Consider the following hypothetical sequence for comparing Religion designated as $(+F_B)$ and Politics designated as $(--F_B)$. The value of "$_B$" will represent the given factors social influence.

Consider the following formula based on the hypothetical values for a Progressive Modern Country.

$F_A = (+F_4) + (--F_7)$

$\therefore F_A = --F_3$

As can be noted the hypothetical society has a stronger linguistic leaning toward Politics than to Religion. In a society of this nature, socio--dialects can be expected to arise through terminology used by marginalised social groups.

Next consider a hypothetical society in which older traditions and beliefs hold sway.

$F_A = (+F_9) + (--F_4)$

$\therefore F_A = +F_5$

In this hypothetical country a local religion or system of beliefs holds power and much of the linguistic influence comes through this vector. The power of religion in such influence (Iannaccone) and in others areas is not to be overlooked.

Dialects are likely to arise from groups where the common or state religion is not their medium of worship and may be directly influenced by the liturgy and terminology of their minority religion.

The greater the final number, the greater the influence of that factor will be, in turn, the level of freedom in association to opposing ideas will decrease. A value of ten would be either a blatant authoritarian state, dictatorship or an error in analysis.

In the rare case that no given or compared factors produce dominance in any area (this is nigh on impossible and such a result would likely indicate either an error in the data collection or incomplete data) the formula will be expressed as $\therefore F_A = F_\emptyset$ where Ø is the standard linguistic notation for zero.

$F_A = F_\emptyset$ would therefore represent a country in perfect social balance in regard to the compared factors.

$F_A = (+F_B) + (--F_B)$ serves to give an approximate trend per social factors and while not being infallible provides insight into potential problematic factors within a society.

It differs from Newton's Third Law in that one sector produces dominance even while resistance is present. The "mass" to use physics terminology, will then be the sector having the largest numerical representation via the equation.

The primary aim of this equation then is to understand the semantic element within any given piece of writing, however within the context of the language and should be contrasted only with another form of the same language or find the trend within a single piece of literature of speech.

There is however the possibility that the semantic encoding within a piece of literature/speech can be misinterpreted by the second party that is to say the listener (Lewis). Poor choice of semantics in association with the syntactical delivery is therefore a powerfully detrimental force when communicating between two parties. There are underlying factors that could be the cause:

A semantic shift in the localised use of a word, phrase or structure.

A propagandic ulterior motive as in 'Strategic Semantics'.

There are five essential features in play during any communicative situation (Jakobson);

Function	Orientation Towards
Informational	Subject/ matter
Expressive	speaker/listener
Directive	listener/ reader
Phatic	Channel of communication
Aesthetic	message

Of these, the expressive, directive and phatic functions greatly influence the social roles of language and its interpretation. A writer or speaker or yet anyone else who when expressing feelings or perceived rather than actual facts affects the emotional response of the listeners either positively or negatively.

As Leech points out on pp. 50;

"*Whenever language is loaded toward or against a given set of attitudes, there is a danger of confusion, unless the addressee is able to distinguish between the conceptual and affective content of the message.*"

Indeed, if the speaker himself/herself is not able to distinguish the reality of a matter the listeners can not be expected to understand either. In this case, the listeners will hypothetically take two possible courses of interpretation;

The message communicated is unclear and appears to be without basis or is irrelevant to me as an individual. I am unable to take in all the facts but feel I understand the main gist of the message which is important.
The second line of reasoning can be of serious social detriment when the interpretation is rendered to encourage ideas or actions that are of an anti-social nature. "What the speaker

said" can therefore become grounds for the extremist or anti-social activities that follow and will be seen by those who interpret it as such, as a form of justification of the given action.

A worse situation is where the speaker purposely and clearly encodes socially degraded semantics ie. 'violence is necessary, no mercy for the enemy' type reasonings. This is ultimately solely designed to elevate the speaker, his cause or another social factor above all else, a proverbial 'rallying of the troops'.

There is a strong danger that the actual semantics of a word will be ignored in favour of the associative meaning or its affective connotation. This is spectacularly the case in words dealing with social groupings, especially words relating to nationalism, politics or religion.

The Naudé Hypothesis can therefore be used as a tool for predicting future trends nationally or globally based on printed or spoken material and can determine to what degree these are pure propaganda.

In conclusion, facilitated by the given facts and the model for function it can be said that the Naudé Hypothesis is significantly rooted in its application so as to be used as a pilot model for further studies. The overall ability of the hypothesis to pinpoint trends within language use and to find the underlying issues within the semantics of a given text make it one of several valuable tools for any linguist. It is hoped that this formula will assist in clarifying further writing within the field of linguistics and guarantee the continued linguistic rights of all people.

$$F_A = (+F_B) + (-F_B)$$

Meaning:

Dominant Right Leaning

$$\therefore F_A = +F_B$$

$$\therefore F_A = -F_B$$

Dominant Left Leaning

Figure: The Hypothetical relationship between forces.

Bibliography:
Newton, I.,ed. 1729; "*Principia*" p20 Volume 1,

Leech, G., 1974. *SEMANTICS*, Harmondsworth: Penguin Books

Ricento, T. ed., 2009. *An introduction to language policy: Theory and method.* John Wiley & Sons.

Wodak, R. ed., 1989. *Language, power and ideology: Studies in political discourse* (Vol. 7). John Benjamins Publishing.

Shohamy, E.G., 2006. *Language policy: Hidden agendas and new approaches.* Psychology Press.

Rannut, M., 1994. *Linguistic human rights: Overcoming linguistic discrimination* (Vol. 67). Walter de Gruyter.

Jakobson, R. 1960 *Linguistics and Poetics.* In Seboek, T.A(ed), Style in Language, Cambridge, Mass, MIT Press

Iannaccone, L.R., 2003. Looking backward: A cross-national study of religious trends. *Unpublished working paper, George Mason University, July.*

Lewis, G.M., 1987. Misinterpretation of Amerindian Information as a Source of Error on Euro-American Maps. *Annals of the Association of American Geographers*, *77*(4), pp.542-563.

Berk, R.A., 1983. An introduction to sample selection bias in sociological data. *American Sociological Review*, pp.386-398.

Hayakama ,S.I. 1964, *Language in Thought and Action*, 2nd Edition, New York; Harcourt, Brace

YOUR KNOWLEDGE HAS VALUE

- We will publish your bachelor's and master's thesis, essays and papers

- Your own eBook and book - sold worldwide in all relevant shops

- Earn money with each sale

Upload your text at www.GRIN.com and publish for free